TWO

ONE ACT PLAYS

TWO

ONE ACT PLAYS

by

Robert Goodier

Contact the author at Robbiegood@hotmail.com
or Robthewriter@hotmail.co.uk

First published October 2013

ISBN : 978-291-58165-2

Other Stage plays by Robert Goodier

Murderous Intentions	ISBN: 978-1-4709-3603-7
Ghost Of Thornley Hall	ISBN: 978-1-4716-3653-0
Family Revelations	ISBN: 978-1-2910-3231-4
Perfect Suspect	ISBN: 978-1-4717-6672-9
To Be Announced	ISBN: 978-1-291-31551-6

Preface **Two one act plays**

Hello reader, I hope that you enjoy the two plays that are in this book that I entered for two "Drama Association Of Wales" One Act Play Competitions in 2008 and 2010. The first prize was £100 and publication of the winning play. The premise behind the competition was to submit a short – up to 50 minutes play with a minimum of 2 characters. So, with that challenge I wrote the two plays that are in this book. And before you ask – no, I didn't win either competition!

So, having salvaged them from the hard drive of a rapidly malfunctioning computer I have decided to publish these short plays so the world can enjoy them and possibly stage them in the future.

The first play "Deceit In Love" is a "two hander" and follows a couple celebrating their anniversary at their favourite restaurant over a number of years. It is partly based on circumstances that I have lived through; although the play is a work of fiction.

The second play "She's Off Her Face(book)" is completely fictional, but based on truth! The truth being the fact that I was addicted to Facebook for eight months and ballooned in weight into the bargain! Though for "artistic licence" I've twisted the tale a little. That's all I'm saying about that play!

Anyhoo, the main point is the fact that I like these two plays and I will never publish anything that I think is "naff", and that is the main reason why these two short plays have been published. The other reason is the fact that no publisher will publish what I've published!

As I always say "enjoy". (I don't know why, I need a new word!)

Robert Goodier (October 2013)

CONTENTS

DECEIT IN LOVE pages 11-36

SHE'S OFF HER FACE(BOOK) pages 38-65

DECEIT IN LOVE

SCENE ONE RESTAURANT (3rd anniversary 2009)

Simone and Roger are sitting lovingly at their table. The meal was excellent and they are content. Their plates and coffee cups are awaiting collection.

SIMONE That was lovely Roger, I'm full to bursting.
ROGER *(proudly)* It was a fantastic meal. I've never had a gammon steak like it before; it wasn't too salty and it wasn't to dry. It was magnificent.
SIMONE *(Amused)* Don't be silly Roger, it always tastes like that. Why don't you be more adventurous when we go out for meals?
ROGER *(In mock astonishment)* Try something other than gammon? You must be kidding. Though on our fourth anniversary I may try that ten ounce beef steak; it does look appetising.
SIMONE *(sarcastic)* Beef steak eh? Don't go overboard will you?
ROGER Well, if we were to compare portion sizes I think I would rather have a meal that fills the whole plate than the meal you had which looked like a dead gold fish in the middle of your plate, *garnished* with something green. I didn't know goldfish ate broccoli.
SIMONE It wasn't a goldfish, it was Mackerel. I'm eating healthily since my doctor told me I had high blood pressure and I was two stone overweight.
ROGER Everyone has high blood pressure at some point and you're not overweight; I like you as you are.
SIMONE You might like me because my tits are getting bigger and you've got more to handle when we're in bed; but I'm getting a spare tyre that's matching yours and it's time that it went.
ROGER *(Happily tapping his tummy)* What can I say? It's a combination of eating well, a great job, a fantastic woman and contentment.
SIMONE That might be so Roger, but since we've been together you've put on three stone in weight.
ROGER *(smiling)* That's one stone for each year we've been together.*(Simone looks at him with disdain)* what? What's that look for?
SIMONE I don't want you getting big, I want the lithe, taut, firm body that I couldn't keep my hands off. If you continue at this rate you'll be twenty stone in four years. I bought you a gym membership for your birthday and you haven't been yet have you?
ROGER *(defensively)* I have been.

SIMONE *(rebuking)* Only to sign in and have a programme worked out for you. Honestly, what a waste of money!
ROGER I'd go if you had joined as well. I mean, we could have had a joint membership for another forty pounds and we could have trained together; as well as sharing the sauna and Jacuzzi. We could be sweaty together.
SIMONE *(firmly)* We could have, but when I signed you up they didn't have any special offers like that. But that's not the point; you haven't been *have* you? So that's a waste of three hundred pounds.
ROGER Okay, I'll give it a go, I'll start next week, but only if you join and train with me.
SIMONE *(Sighing)* If you insist.
ROGER *(Changing the subject)* Anyway, we've not come here for an argument, we've come here to celebrate our third anniversary.
SIMONE *(Smiling)* I know, three wonderful and happy years to a wonderful man who makes me very happy.
ROGER *(Touched)* That's a very sweet thing to say Simone. Thank you

He leans over the table and kisses her. First a peck on the lips, then a full on kiss with passion

SIMONE *(catching her breath)* Your kisses always make me tingle.
ROGER Your lips are irresistible, how can I refuse to kiss them?
SIMONE *(clutching his hand)* You charmer!
ROGER I must be doing something right, it's our third anniversary *(raises his glass)* A toast to the most sexy, gorgeous, loving, alluring woman that I have the privilege to know

They clink glasses

SIMONE And here is to the hunkiest, fittest, wittiest, fantasticalist lover I have ever had. *(they clink glasses again)*
ROGER Fantasicalist? What kind of word is that?
SIMONE It's **a** word I've made up especially for you. I think it describes the way you make love to me rather well.
ROGER Hmm, as long as you don't say it when we do make love.
SIMONE *(happily)* I've bought you a present.
ROGER *(Surprised)* Oh, you didn't have to.
SIMONE Of course I did. Plus I'm not having you pay for such a wonderful meal and this fantastic weekend in this five star hotel either; I'm paying half.
ROGER *(sternly)* No.

SIMONE No?
ROGER No, it's my treat and you really didn't half to buy me anything.
SIMONE *(Producing the present)* Here.

He takes it from her, his expression can't stay stern, he breaks into a smile. Excitedly he rips open the beautiful wrapping paper.

ROGER Nice paper.
SIMONE It was till you got your mitts on it.
ROGER *(Disappointed, he hides it with a smile)* Oh, a mobile phone; it's, err great.
SIMONE *(stunned at the rebuff)* What's the matter with it? You're always complaining that you can never contact me at work and now you can. I'll be 'in when I'm out', as it were. Plus it's got a video screen so you can download all the porn you want and watch it on the train when you go to work. *(She laughs, he doesn't)* I'm joking; you don't need porn when you've got me. *(worried)* Don't you like it?
ROGER *(disappointed)* It's okay, but it wasn't what I expected.
SIMONE And what did you expect considering that you didn't know I was going to give you a present?

Roger produces a case and Simone takes it. She understands the intention.

Is this a ring?
ROGER Open it.

She does, it's a beautiful emerald and gold ring.

Try it on. I know it's your size and I know you like emeralds. *(Eagerly)* Go on.
SIMONE *(Putting it on a finger on her right hand)* Is this the ring that I've been looking at every time I go into town?
ROGER *(Pleased)* It is, do you like?
SIMONE *(Touched, kisses him)* I'm lost for words. Thank you.
ROGER My pleasure.
SIMONE But it's nearly two hundred pounds, are you sure?
ROGER Of course I'm sure. If I wasn't I would have bought you some Marks and Spencer's knickers and a bottle of 'Eau de Toilet', or whatever it is you like.
SIMONE *(Admiring it)* Are you sure that you can afford it?

ROGER Of course I can. *(takes her hand)* There is a more ulterior motive behind this ring you know.
SIMONE *(Tensing)* There is?

Roger puts the ring on her wedding finger and gets down on one knee.

ROGER Simone Tomlinson, will you marry me?

He smiles hopefully; Simone is embarrassed and looks around to see whose looking. Finally, she looks at his face, moves her hands away and takes off the ring, placing it on the table. Roger is heartbroken as he sits back in his seat. He sadly stares at the ring.

ROGER Why not this time? We've been together for three years.
SIMONE I'm not ready.
ROGER *(Amazed)* Not ready? How do you work that out? You don't want to get married to me, is that it?
SIMONE Don't talk rot Roger. I do love you, I really do, but I don't want to be married and tied down that's all. I like things the way they are between us.
ROGER Well I don't, I want to make an honest woman of you.
SIMONE *(Laughing)* I'm flattered that you want to, but I told you right from the first time that we met that I don't want to marry, didn't I?
ROGER So?
SIMONE And I meant it *(she takes his hands, looking directly at him)* why won't you listen to me, hmm? I like what we have, I like seeing you, I like going out with you, I like the fact that we're not in each other's hair twenty four seven.
ROGER Well maybe I'm not happy with things. It's always your say when I go to your house and stay the night; it's always you who calls me when *you* want to go out. Every time I suggest that you come and stay at mine or go somewhere you always have something else to do. What do you think I am? Your lap dog or something? Some kind of 'sex slave' that you can call on at a moment's notice when you want to be seduced? Just click your fingers and I'll come running. Am I just at your beck and call when it suits you?
SIMONE If I seem to remember, I was at your beck and call when your girlfriend was in Scotland every other weekend.
ROGER And as I said at the time, when I met you we were breaking up, things between us overlapped that's all.
SIMONE *(angrily)* I don't believe this.

ROGER *(aghast)* What don't you believe?
SIMONE *(Rising)* I'm going home.
ROGER *(Shocked)* But, but you can't!
SIMONE *(firmly)* But I can and I will. Listen Roger; I do love you, but I don't want to be married to you. I know three years for you is a long time in a relationship and it probably is for me too; but why spoil it by marrying? Why make it formal?
ROGER I just think it's a good idea. At least it shows you that I love you enough to consider marrying you, doesn't it? Give me some credit for that won't you?
SIMONE I will and I appreciate it, you just surprised me that's all.
ROGER Do you like the ring?
SIMONE Of course I do, but I think that you're going a little over the top that's all.
ROGER Why can't I buy you a ring? It's just a little something to say how much I love you that's all.
SIMONE I know that you love me Roger, but you didn't have to buy me such an expensive ring.
ROGER Well, let's just forget the meaning behind it then; just promise me that you'll wear it for me.
SIMONE Of course I will, it's beautiful *(admires it, she smiles at Roger)*
ROGER *(Tentatively)* So, er, are you leaving then?
SIMONE *(surprised)* Leaving?
ROGER A second ago you were leaving. Have you changed your mind?
SIMONE *(Sits)* No, I'm not leaving, and I was just being a little hot headed that's all. I really appreciate this weekend and I hope that it will be a completely dirty one; if you're up for it that is.
ROGER *(lustily)* I'm up for it now if you must know.
SIMONE *(Playfully slapping him)* You horny sod! And in public too!**ROGER** Come on, let's go to our room, there's a bottle of champagne and a big box of Celebration chocolates to munch through while we watch the adult channel.

They both rise and exit giggling as. . . .

SIMONE *(suddenly remembering)* Did you bring the Viagra?

The lights dim

SCENE TWO Same restaurant, one year later. (4th anniversary)

Once again they are sat at the same table.

ROGER *(Toasting Simone)* To Simone, who gets lovelier every year.
SIMONE *(Toasting Roger)* To Roger, the love of my life who has lost four stone in weight since he finally started going to the gym and is my sexy hunk of love. Cheers *(they clink glasses and drink)*
ROGER *(amazed)* I can't believe it was a year since we were here last; where has the time gone?
SIMONE *(Guessing)* Having fun? Getting older? Being in the gym for five hours at a time? I don't know, you tell me.
ROGER I wasn't in the gym for five hours at a time, so don't exaggerate. *(Proudly)* But I do look good for it don't I?
SIMONE *(Grinning)* You certainly do. I'm so glad that you *finally* started to go to the gym; it's taken years off you, not to mention the inches.
ROGER It was bloody hard work I can tell you, but the results speak for themselves. And I must say that you are looking quite sexy these days; I could eat you right now.
SIMONE *(Amused)* Calm down Roger, we haven't had desert yet.
ROGER I can't help it. Since you got that promotion to head librarian, or whatever you call it, you've simply glowed. It suites you, it really does.
SIMONE *(Proudly)* I'm glad that you have noticed, because the students certainly have. Apparently library loans have gone up thirty two percent this last semester and I'm at a loss to wonder why.
ROGER Maybe it's because of the new look, sexy you.
SIMONE Or it could be down to the new assistant Melanie who wears the shortest skirts and tiniest, tightest t-shirts that I've ever seen.
ROGER *(Feigning ignorance)* Melanie? Who's she then?
SIMONE *(Aghast)* Don't tell me that you haven't notice her when you've been waiting for me?
ROGER *(Innocently)* I can't say that I have to be honest. Is she the one with the perfect teeth?
SIMONE *(Playfully slapping him)* You know damn well who I'm talking about, so stop pretending to be dumb about it.
ROGER *(feigns remembering)* Ah, I know who you mean now. Is she the one who is twenty one and comes from Belgium?

SIMONE You know perfectly well who I'm talking about. Anyway, this is our fourth anniversary, so I forbid you to talk about any younger, more attractive women than me. Comprehend?
ROGER *(Saluting mockingly)* Yes ma'am.
SIMONE You can be *so* sarcastic, do you know that.
ROGER *(Saluting again)* Yes ma'am.
SIMONE I give up, I really do.
ROGER *(Contrite)* Sorry ma'am.
SIMONE *(annoyed)* Stop being so bloody childish will you?
ROGER Okay, okay, blimey, where's your sense of fun nowadays?
SIMONE Sorry, I'm just a little tired that's all. *(Brightening)* Anyway, it's time for us to exchange our customary anniversary gifts to each other. So what have you got for me? *(looks hopefully at Roger)*
ROGER *(Dryly)* You want an anniversary present off me? Simone, how could you have the nerve? After all I've bought for you this year?
SIMONE *(Teasing)* Oh? And what did you buy me this year? Remind me?

Roger coughs and produces a notepad from his jacket pocket and leafs through it. Simone is aghast

Are you keeping a list? How dare you! *(she playfully slaps his wrists)*
ROGER Erm, let me see. In April we went to stay in Scotland for four days, in July we had that weekend in Dublin getting very drunk . . . . oh and in September I bought you that very nice Mini Cooper that you like so much.

He puts the notepad back in his pocket and looks smugly at her astonished face.

SIMONE Are you being serious?
ROGER Well I am sorry, but you are dating an accountant. It's a habit of mine, I do apologise.
SIMONE So what are you doing then? Making notes so you can claim back the V.A.T?
ROGER I hadn't thought of that! Good idea. *(Writes it down in his notepad)*
SIMONE Oh come on Roger, stop teasing; what have you got me for our anniversary? *(flutters her eyes at him)*
ROGER I love it when you do that.
SIMONE *(Impatiently)* Well?

After a moment he proudly hands her an envelope. Puzzled, she takes it, opens it, reads the contents and is stunned to know what to say.

Are you serious? How much has this cost you?
ROGER It doesn't matter, what does matter is whether you want to go or not.
SIMONE Well of course I'll go, but it must have cost you a fortune. have you 'accounted' for it?
ROGER Money is no object when it comes to giving you an anniversary present. So, do you want to go or not?
SIMONE Of course I'll go to New York with you, I'd be mad not to.
ROGER *(kisses her)* That's okay then. Now, shall we retire to our room? I want to make mad, horny love to you.
SIMONE *(Sternly)* No, not tonight.
ROGER *(Taken aback)* No?
SIMONE No. I want you to make love to me with the passion of a man that has lost five stone at the gym and the agility and staying power of an eighteen year old.
ROGER Sorry, I can't manage that, But I can manage to make love to you like a guy that has lost *four* stone in weight and has the staying power of a seventeen year old.
SIMONE Okay, but I must warn you, that I'm nearly forty and reaching my sexual peak, so I will most likely wear you out.
ROGER That's fine with me.
SIMONE *(Rising and taking his hand)* Then why are we wasting time here then? There's a king size bed waiting for us upstairs.

They both exit, giggling like a pair of teenagers.

SCENE THREE. Restaurant (5th anniversary)

Roger is sat at their table alone. He has consumed two bottles of wine and pours the remainder of a third into his glass. He checks his watch and drums on the table impatiently while looking hopefully towards the door. Finally a flustered Simone arrives and sits down.

SIMONE *(apologetic)* I am *so* sorry that I'm late.
ROGER *(sarcastic)* Only by three quarters of an hour.

SIMONE Well I'm sorry okay? I couldn't leave the library because there was an alarm fault; I had to stay until it was sorted. I did leave you a voice-mail message you know.
ROGER I got the missed calls from you, but I never got a voice-mail message.
SIMONE *(agitated)* Well I did sent you a message, check your phone.
ROGER I haven't got it with me, sorry. I left it at work because I came straight here.
SIMONE *(exasperated)* What's the point of having that mobile phone I bought for you if you don't have it with you? Anyway, you've been busy I see.
ROGER What do you mean?
SIMONE *(rebuking)* Two bottles of wine? I hope you're not going back to your bad old ways.
ROGER Don't worry, I'm not going to turn into a raging alcoholic if that's what you think.
SIMONE I wasn't suggesting anything of the sort. Have you ordered?
ROGER No, I was waiting for you. *(he picks up the menu)*
SIMONE *(Concerned)* Hey, I couldn't help it. I can't just leave work while there's an alarm fault. How would it look if I upped and left and then the library got ransacked or something? It would be gross misconduct and I'd be sacked for leaving my station. Surely you understand?
ROGER *(beat, understands)* Of course I do. I'm sorry; I've had a bad day.
SIMONE You and me both then. *(she picks up the menu and takes a breath)* Wow!
ROGER *(surprised)* What?
SIMONE Are we in the same restaurant?
ROGER What do you mean?
SIMONE Well, for one, the menu has gone all French and the prices have more than trebled.
ROGER Oh, that's because the hotel changed owners in May. Two premiership footballers bought the place. But don't worry about the cost.
SIMONE *(Curious)* Oh yes? Why?
ROGER I spoke to the *new* manager and told him that we always come here for our anniversary and that this one, being our fifth was an extra special one. So . . . . I managed to get us fifty percent off everything *and* we've got the honeymoon suite.
SIMONE *(Stunned)* You've got us what?

ROGER Well, as a skilled negotiator as well as being a highly trained accountant . . . . *(smiles)* well, let's just say that our fifth anniversary has cost us practically . . . . nothing.
SIMONE *(Puzzled)* I don't understand.
ROGER I got us here for two nights for the price of one and the meal is on the house. *(He sits back, smugly)*
SIMONE *(puzzled)* How?
ROGER I know the manager; his wife is my best client. I got us a discount in return for some jiggling of his wife's business account.
SIMONE You're talking in riddles. What do you mean?
ROGER His wife owns a florist shop and she owes sixteen thousand pounds to the tax-man. If I fiddle her books I can save her that money and get the tax-man to repay her four grand in overpaid taxes.
SIMONE *(impressed)* How? Can you do that?
ROGER *(smugly)* It's my job; it's what I'm best at.
SIMONE *(unsure)* Well, so long as it's legal.
ROGER Everything I do is legal. I just spotted a few loopholes that's all. So it's a favour for a favour really.
SIMONE Well I'm impressed. I bet you could do the books for Mike Burns. I'm sure he'd be extremely grateful, being as he is a freelance lecturer.
ROGER *(annoyed)* Oh here we go.
SIMONE *(puzzled)* What?
ROGER Him again.
SIMONE What about him?
ROGER It's funny how you always manage to sneak him into everything that we talk about isn't it?
SIMONE He happens to be a very good friend of mine
ROGER And I'm not?
SIMONE Oh this is impossible! Why do you get so annoyed whenever I mention his name? He's just a work colleague that's all.
ROGER Is he? The only things that you have talked about these last three months are how pissed off you are at the library; how hard done to you are because you didn't get that sideways promotion; and him *(he angrily spits out 'him')*
SIMONE *(confused)* Are you going to be like this all night?
ROGER Like what?
SIMONE A child? You're supposed to be the 'professional, cool headed accountant' aren't you?
ROGER Who said that?

SIMONE You do, all the time. So stop going on about what I work with; I mean, I don't go on about you talking about that secretary of yours do I?
ROGER I do not!
SIMONE The fact that she's 'twenty six got great legs and a figure to die for'; do I talk about her? Do I?
ROGER No you don't talk about her and I don't either! Bloody hell Simone, what's got into you? Of course I've noticed her; I wouldn't be a man if I didn't. But I didn't employ her, my boss did and she's not my exclusive secretary, all my colleagues share her.
SIMONE 'Share her'? You make her sound like a whore!
ROGER Well she isn't a 'whore'. And I could very well talk about her, what with all the mistakes she makes I could talk about her a lot, because each day she does something so unbelievably stupid! But how would that sound to you? How would that make you feel?
SIMONE *(indignant)* So you've noticed her have you? And how would you compare her to me? Go on, tell me.

Roger looks at her, amazed and stunned, he can't answer that question.

I take it by the silence that you do compare her to me. In what way? Her legs? Figure? I noticed that night I picked you up from work that she doesn't wear a bra, are her tits nicer than mine?
ROGER *(amazed)* What the hell has brought this on?
SIMONE You brought this on; going on about Mike Burns all the time!
ROGER I don't go on about him, you do. I only told you about the fact you mention him all the time that's all. For fucks sake Simone, take a chill pill will you!
SIMONE *(Glares at him)* Wow! I'm stunned. That's the first time you have ever swore at me.
ROGER *(Disbelief, then sarcastic)* Oh, I am so terribly sorry *darling*.

Both glare at each other, there isn't going to be a stand down. Simone pours herself a large drink and drains half the glass.

ROGER Steady old girl, don't drink so much so quickly, its twenty five quid a bottle you know.
SIMONE *(insulted)* Old girl am I? Oh, sorry I'm not in my twenties and don't show all the men my tits. Would you like me to go around not wearing a bra?

ROGER Don't talk rot Simone; besides, my boss told her off for not wearing one and now she wears a bra, which I have to say is a vast improvement.
SIMONE What do you mean?
ROGER *(happily)* Well, for one, it enhances the look of them, they look nicer, more rounded.

He laughs because he has made a 'Joke', Simone doesn't find it funny

SIMONE You're a pig Roger.
ROGER It was a joke. Good grief Simone, what's up with you tonight? You're like a bloody grizzly bear!
SIMONE I'm sorry Roger, it's been a hell week. I nearly didn't come tonight.
ROGER *(Lavishly)* Well you will 'come' later, I'll see to that.
SIMONE *(repulsed)* Don't be so crude Roger, it doesn't be 'come' you.

Roger is stunned and ashamed by his comment, he realises something has changed between them.

ROGER Fair enough. Sorry Simone if I come across as a dog on heat; it's the way you affect me that's all. You're the only woman that I've truly loved you know.
SIMONE *(Realising he's being honest)* I know Roger, I know. And I'm sorry I'm being so touchy tonight, it's just been a really, really bad day at work and I shouldn't take it out on you. Forgive me?
ROGER *(Unsure)* Of course I do. I've never seen you like this before; maybe a pampering session will relax you.
SIMONE *(intrigued)* A pampering session? What do you mean?
ROGER *(Proudly)* I've got you a full two hour massage, and a nail, hair and makeover for your anniversary present. It's worth one hundred and fifty quid. And you can have it any time from now. Though the voucher is valid for one year, so you'd better be quick.

He hands it over to her and she cries. He is stunned

Darling, what's the matter? Don't you like it?
SIMONE I do, I really do. You're so thoughtful and generous.

ROGER *(Proudly)* I think you can definitely say that I am! Although I know you had your heart set on that diamond ring you saw in the half price jewellers but it had gone when I called in.
SIMONE Oh forget the ring Roger, this is fantastic! You always seem to know what I need and you time it so nicely too! I'm sorry that I've been so horrible to you this evening.

She kisses him on the cheek, Roger is disappointed that it wasn't on the lips

ROGER It's my pleasure Simone *(trails off, expectant of his present from her to him)*
SIMONE *(Fishing around in her handbag)* The present I've got you looks like I'm a cheapskate compared to yours, it's in here somewhere.
ROGER Nice bag, I didn't buy you that did I?
SIMONE *(lying)* Err, no, I got it in the sales. Ah, here it is.

She produces a tiny well wrapped gift and proudly gives it to a suspicious Roger who doesn't take his eyes off the handbag.

(happily) Go on, open it.

He does so and it is a CD of his favourite band. He doesn't hide his disappointment.

ROGER Wow, err, thanks, that's err, wonderful
SIMONE What's wrong with it? You like them don't you?
ROGER Of course I do, it's great. Thanks *(he kisses her quickly).*
SIMONE It's not just a CD you know.
ROGER *(in a huff)* It looks like one to me Simone.
SIMONE *(Excited)* Open it up!

He does so and gasps.

Now what do you think?
ROGER *(overwhelmed)* Wow! That is fantastic!
SIMONE Two tickets to see them in Liverpool at the summer pops. When I saw them on the internet I couldn't believe it myself, especially as you're always telling me that they last played in the UK in nineteen eighty nine. *(happily)* So, what do you think?

ROGER *(flattered)* Wow! This is fantastic. I love it! It's possibly the best gift I've ever had!

He kisses her on the cheek, then on the lips, but Simone doesn't want to be kissed. He notices but hides his disappointment.

It's been sold out for months, wow; it must have cost you a few quid
SIMONE Don't worry about the cost, I'm so glad you like them.
ROGER *(excited)* I more than like them! I'm going to have to dust of my old denim jacket now, that's if it still fits!
SIMONE Well if it doesn't, I'll buy you a new one.
ROGER Oh no, you can't do that. A new jacket will stand out like a sore thumb at this gig, it would be like wearing socks with sandals. No, my old jacket has badges and sew on patches all over it. I sometimes think that if I took them off the jacket would collapse because they've been on it for so long! You know how old I was when I last saw this band?
SIMONE I have no idea.
ROGER *(excited)* I was nineteen! Nineteen years old! It was the last time they played Britain before the drug busts and their split *(he looks at the tickets in awe)* and now they're back!

He stands up and mimics a rock guitarist. Simone is embarrassed. Suddenly her mobile rings; she checks to see who it is and stops it ringing.

SIMONE *(guiltily)* Sorry about that.
ROGER *(Sitting)* Who was that?
SIMONE *(shrugging)* It doesn't matter, I've put it on voice-mail.
ROGER Well turn it off, I'm not having phones ruining our evening.
SIMONE I can't.
ROGER Why not?
SIMONE I'm on call – sorry.
ROGER *(suspiciously)* What do you mean 'on call'?
SIMONE *(resigned)* It's my turn to be on call in case the alarm goes off again. I'm sorry.
ROGER *(annoyed)* How could you be on call tonight of all nights? You know what tonight is don't you?
SIMONE Of course I do. I explained it to my boss, but she wasn't having any of it. Besides, I have it sorted; Melanie said she'd cover for me if I was unavailable.
ROGER How will Melanie know that you're unavailable?

SIMONE *(Lying)* I'll just have to tell her, remind her, that's all. I'll ring her.
ROGER *(Suspicious)* Ring her then.

Simone is suddenly unsure if Roger has seen through her lie. She rings 'Melanie'.

SIMONE *(To Roger)* It's ringing. Oh hi Melanie, yes I did get a phone call. Listen, will you cover for me liked we arranged? I know it's a pain, but I wouldn't ask you if tonight wasn't important you know that . . . . yes I'll pay for your taxi's, just get me the receipt. Oh thank you, you've saved my bacon tonight, I'll return the favour when it's your turn I promise. Bye then, bye.

With a sigh of relief she cancels the call, puts the phone in her handbag, smiles at the doubtful Roger.

ROGER Thank you for that, I'd hate the evening to be spoiled by that blasted library alarm.
SIMONE Don't worry, Melanie isn't one to go blabbing to the hierarchy, she knows better. Anyway, come on, let's get on with the evening, I'm ravenous.
ROGER *(Relenting)* So am I *(looks through the menu)*
SIMONE *(teasing)* Guess what I'm going to order?
ROGER *(knowingly)* I can't, do tell.
SIMONE I'll give you a clue – it's one of the few dishes that I can pronounce.

Roger studies the menu and smiles

ROGER *(understanding)* Are you having lemon or an egg with your gammon?
SIMONE Ooh egg, definitely.
ROGER *(sarcastic)* That's definitely how to have a gammon steak. Now how about the wine?
SIMONE *(teasing more)* Wine? How about a pint of Guinness?
ROGER *(stunned)* Guinness? I am surprised! Two pints of Guinness it is!

He clicks his fingers for a waiter to come over and attend to them.

Have you give any thought to what we talked about the other night?

SIMONE *(seriously)* Yes, yes I have.
ROGER *(Expectantly)* And. . . . ?
SIMONE Yes, yes I will marry you Roger. I feel that the time is right now.
ROGER *(Overwhelmed)* Oh Simone, I'm so happy! You know I will make an honest woman out of you.
SIMONE *(Disappointed)* Really?
ROGER Of course I will; now you are my betrothed. I think we need more than just Guinness. Waiter, a bottle of your finest most expensive champagne please.

The lights fade as they chat happily to each other.

RESTAUARANT 6th anniversary

They are sat at their regular table, but relations between them are very frosty.

SIMONE You not having gammon tonight?
ROGER No, I thought I'd be more adventurous and try a grilled steak.
SIMONE *(pointedly)* I suppose that's good dear, but you really should stop, or cut back on the crappy food that you eat nowadays, you're looking quite chubby again.
ROGER *(hurt)* Really? Well you're no Kate Moss are you? I suppose you're going to order scampi again are you?
SIMONE *(irritated)* And what's wrong with scampi? It's quite a healthy food is sea food.
ROGER *(scoffing)* How can food that has been polluted with oil from boats and sewage be healthy for you?
SIMONE *(Snapping)* What is wrong with you tonight?
ROGER You know what is wrong; do I have to repeat myself?
SIMONE I don't see why you are so bothered about it, you've been at that company for nine years, if you're made redundant. . . .
ROGER *(Interrupting)* It isn't 'redundancy', the company are downsizing that's all.
SIMONE Well, whatever you want to call it then; look, enjoy it, if they let you go you could always go freelance. You've always said that you would do that anyway.
ROGER It doesn't matter now does it? I'm forty four; I'm past it. Who's going to employ a forty four year old eh?

SIMONE Don't be daft! Of course you'll get another job, you're good at it aren't you?
ROGER *(Unhappy)* I suppose so *(he picks up his glass and plays with it)*
SIMONE There's something else on your mind isn't there?
ROGER Well, to be quite honest, there is.
SIMONE *(Concerned, take his hands)* What is it? You can tell me, I'm here for you, you know that.
ROGER *(Snatching his hands away, annoyed)* Are you?
SIMONE *(surprised)* What do you mean?
ROGER What do I mean? You and that Mike guy, that's what I mean!
SIMONE Oh you're impossible, you know that!
ROGER Am I? How come he's always with you? How come he always seems to be everywhere that we go? It doesn't matter if it's the theatre, cinema, or a pub; he's always there. And if he isn't there you're always talking about him. And, and worse than that, he was at our fucking engagement party and you were all over him like a rash! And don't tell me that there's nothing going on between you and that you are just 'good friends' because we've had that argument already! (*He stands, ready for leaving, angry)*
SIMONE Sit down will you, you're causing a scene
ROGER Our *engagement* party, how could you Simone?
SIMONE Listen, Roger, sit down, will you please? I have something to tell you that you will not like. So, sit down, please.
ROGER *(Sits down)* Okay, I'm all ears. Tell me.
SIMONE *(Suddenly unsure)* This isn't an easy thing to tell you. But before I do, I want you to know that I do love you. I always have. . . .
ROGER Ha! I knew it! You do want us to end don't you? I knew it, I knew it! I've been anticipating this for the last few months, and now *(throws his hands up in defeat)*. It's since this Mike guy came on the scene. Isn't it? It's him; I know that he has something to do with it.
SIMONE You're right, Mike has got something to do with what I am going to tell you, but not in the way you think.
ROGER *(Sarcastically)* Ooh, do tell, I know that you have been shagging him. . . .
SIMONE *(firmly)* I have not been shagging him!
ROGER *(raising his voice)* Well what then? If you're not *shagging* him and you are certainly not *shagging* me, then who are you *shagging*?!
SIMONE *(Loses her composure)* I'm not *shagging* anybody, okay?! Why does everything that I do, or we do, revolve around sex?

ROGER Well, if you are *not* shagging him, or me, then you must be shagging somebody, because we certainly haven't done it for nearly three months.

SIMONE It? Three months? You're counting the days since we last 'did it'? Has it ever occurred to you that I may have lost my sex drive? No, that would never cross your mind. Or how about this for a reason - my abortion?

ROGER *(Scoffing)* Your abortion? What the hell has that got to do with it?

SIMONE *(Stunned at his remark)* You heartless bastard! I had that abortion and it hurt like hell! I had four weeks off work sick because I couldn't walk. I bled for weeks and I was in absolute agony! And all you could do was complain that you never got your end away! I don't believe you at times Roger!

ROGER *(contrite)* Okay, I'm sorry! I didn't mean it, it was just frustration talking. I hadn't realised that you were so bad after the abortion. I just put two and two together and assumed that you had gone off me, that's all.

SIMONE *(Laughs, then embraces him)* Don't be silly, Roger. I love you and sex with you is always fantastic. It's been frustrating for me too you know. Being cooped up in bed for weeks longing for you. But I can honestly say that I am not having sex with anybody else, or even Mike, okay? It's taken me longer to recover than I had hoped.

ROGER *(embarrassed laugh)* I'm sorry Simone, I've been an arse haven't I!? I've been so self-centred and selfish. But I did think that it was a coincidence that sex stopped as soon as this Mike guy came onto the scene.

SIMONE Well you can put your mind at rest, I am not having sex with Mike Burns okay. *(She kisses him lightly on the forehead)* Or even you for that matter.

ROGER *(Stunned)* Pardon?

SIMONE *(backtracking)* I was only joking with you, don't be so gullible.

ROGER I wouldn't be if I knew where we now stand. It's not just the great sex that I've missed; it's you. I hardly see you anymore. You're either working at the library till late, or going away on weekend courses. And if it isn't work, you're going out more often with people from work and excluding me. And if it's because I pulled that Mooney at your faculty head, then how many more times can I say I'm sorry?

SIMONE It wasn't the Mooney, she thought it was hilarious.

ROGER Well what is then? Do you know how many times I've seen you in the last six weeks?

SIMONE I don't, but I know that you are going to tell me anyway.

ROGER I've seen you six times. That's all, six times. Once a week. And do you know how many times out of those six we have been out together?*(Simone shrugs)* Once. And that was a party at Bruce's house.
SIMONE What's wrong with that?
ROGER Oh, I'll tell you what's wrong with that. We only stayed at Bruce's for an hour because you had a 'migraine'. I wouldn't mind, we got there at ten o'clock and it was a really rocking party.
SIMONE You didn't have to leave you know.
ROGER Maybe not, but I felt embarrassed there on my own.
SIMONE *(Scoffing)* You weren't on your own though, everybody there at the party were your friends from your Amateur Dramatics Society. So how can you say that?
ROGER It just wouldn't have been the same without you there that's all. I've got used to you being with me everywhere we go. *(Simone tuts and rolls her eyes)* What's that supposed to mean?
SIMONE What?
ROGER Rolling your eyes and tutting?
SIMONE It doesn't mean anything.
ROGER It does, tell me. *(He looks at her thoughtfully)* Do you think that I am becoming clingy?
SIMONE I wouldn't say clingy – more . . . overbearing. Yes, overbearing.
ROGER *(Aghast)* Overbearing?! Is that what I am to you now? 'Overbearing?' All I am trying to do is make sense with what has happened to us lately. You tell me that I am not to worry; you tell me that I am being 'paranoid'; you tell me that nothing is wrong between us. But something is wrong between us . . . and I would be grateful if you put me out of my misery and let me know. Please.

Simone is at a loss what she can say. She has feelings for Roger, but her circumstances have altered dramatically. She hesitates before she answers.

SIMONE *(whispering)* I am really not sure how you will take what I am going to tell you Roger, and I am ashamed that I have led you a merry dance for the last six years . . . .
ROGER *(suspiciously)* Go on. . . .
SIMONE *(Cautiously)* You have every right to be suspicious of Mike Burns. . . . You see – he is still my husband. *(She turns away)*

Roger, puzzled rises, crouching down face to face with Simone who is struggling to control her tears.

ROGER *(Quietly)* I don't understand. When you say 'husband', do you mean, 'ex divorced husband'?
SIMONE No – I mean that he is *still* my husband.
ROGER *(confused)* You are still *married* to him?
SIMONE *(reluctantly)* Yes.

Roger struggles to comprehend what she has just told him. The two of them are in sad silence as they both think about everything they had, everything that they have now lost.

ROGER *(sitting down)* I, I don't understand.
SIMONE What don't you understand? Tomlinson is my maiden name.
ROGER *(stunned)* Maiden name**?!** How can you have been so deceitful? *(She simply shrugs)* We have been together for six years and not *once* have you ever mentioned the fact that you are *married.* How the hell did you manage to keep it from me? How the hell could you have gone through the pretence of having an engagement party with me? How the hell can you live with yourself?
SIMONE *(tearfully)* It wasn't something that I had intended to do. I do want to marry you! You're a fantastic guy Roger.
ROGER *(Sarcastically)* Really? So when where you going to tell me that you were still married? At the altar just before we say 'I do?' On our honeymoon? Or when the police raid our house after a tip off and you get arrested for bigamy?
SIMONE Don't talk rubbish Roger.
ROGER *(aghast)* Me talk rubbish? Well that's rich coming from you! (*He hits the nearest object to him, breaking it, Simone winces)* Six years! Six fucking years we have been together and not once in those six years have you *ever* said you are married or still married. You said that you didn't even have a boyfriend when we met. And what about our engagement? Why did you go through with that if you knew that you were still married? I've been living a lie for six years! All those expensive presents I've bought you! All those weekends away! I've completely wasted my time! And for what? What have I got to show for it?
SIMONE *(remorseful)* This wasn't something that I had planned! I hadn't seen him for eight years and even though he sent me the forms to sign from his solicitors, I ignored them. I ripped them up and placed them in the bin. In my heart I still loved him; I hated him too. I lived in hope that we would get

together and even though I fought it, I hadn't really intended in falling in love with him again . . . .
ROGER *(disbelieving)* Huh . . . What you said didn't make any sense. You still loved him but you didn't intend to 'fall in love with him again'? Don't make me laugh!
SIMONE It's true! Let me tell you something about us. Mike and I met at the University; he was a lecturer and I was a librarian. We hit it off straight away and within six months we were married. It was a silly thing to do I know; but we loved each other and it seemed the right thing to do.
ROGER *(A little calmer)* So, what happened between you?
SIMONE It was a combination of things, and they were all bad. Firstly he was spotted frequently taking a female lecturer out for meals, but claimed they were strictly meeting concerning the curriculum, but I never believed it. Secondly, he was always out till late at night, sometimes till three or four in the morning and he frequently smelled of sex and cigarette smoke. Yet he would always tell me that nobody he worked with smoked and it was the places that they went to that made him smell of it. And it wasn't just cigarette smoke that I could smell, it was cheap perfume too and like a fool I would believe him *(laughs)* Maybe I believed him because I wanted to. I don't really know. Maybe I believed him because I couldn't believe that he could be unfaithful to me. Does that make sense?
ROGER *(nods)* Yes. Carry on, this is most interesting.
SIMONE Anyway, soon after he tells me that he had got a job lecturing in America and it was an immediate start. And that was it, he was off. Taking with him the female lecturer that he denied he wasn't sleeping with. It was so sudden too. Friday we were in bed having the most wonderful sex; Monday he was off on a Jet plane to some god forsaken university in America.
ROGER That, erm, is quite nasty isn't it.
SIMONE Oh yes, and the worse of it *(steels herself)* was the fact that I was pregnant.
ROGER *Pregnant*?
SIMONE *(Nodding)* I had gone to the doctors on the Friday morning and I was itching to tell him, I was so excited! But he wouldn't talk to me; he was very moody. *(Laughs ironically)* And now I know why.
ROGER *(Hugging her)* Oh Simone I am so sorry.

They hug for a minute. She breaks off, looking him straight in the eyes. Roger frowns, though slightly puzzled.

SIMONE I want you both, but I can't and it hurts me.
ROGER It hurts me too. Six years you've deceived me. . . .
SIMONE If he hadn't come back I would have divorced him. My feelings for you have become so confused lately . . .
ROGER *(with a huff)* Huh, I'm not surprised.
SIMONE *(stunned)* Don't be like that.
ROGER Well what do you expect from me? I've had my suspicions about you two for the last few months, now I know why. Did you see him before you casually introduced him to me as "an old friend".
SIMONE *(puzzled)* What do you mean?
ROGER Do you remember the party at Marlene's? I noticed when he arrived you smiling at him.
SIMONE So what? I smiled at everybody there. It was a party; did you expect me to stand in a corner with a sulky face or something?
ROGER Well of course not! But it was the *way* that you smiled at him. As soon as he came into the room you went straight to him. I saw you squeeze his hand; just a slight touch.
SIMONE Well, if you had your suspicions from the moment that I 'smiled and touched his hand'; why then, didn't you say something that night? I mean, it's not like you to miss an opportunity to have a blazing row is it?
ROGER *(amazed)* Why are you suddenly making me out to be argumentative? I just noticed you touching his hand that's all.
SIMONE Look, Roger, it's not my fault that you have had such a loveless upbringing and that you can't understand that two people can be friends and be affectionate with each other; I thought I had got through to you. . .
ROGER *(angrily)* What does that mean? Now you're trying to make me out to be an emotionless monster! Are you trying to drive me insane or something? You're turning and twisting everything that I've told about my parents into a . . . I don't know what you're doing; but I don't like it.
SIMONE *(rises)* I'm not doing anything. I don't know what's come over you lately, but you're not the Roger that I liked, that I do know.
ROGER See? There you go again. Now you're telling me that you don't like me, and that's on top of the emotional cripple that you're making me out to be!
SIMONE *(Walks away)* Oh, you're impossible! I can't talk to you when you're in one of these moods! I'm going home.
ROGER *(Stops her)* Whoa, you're not going anywhere.
SIMONE *(firmly)* I'm going home. Let me go.

ROGER I want answers Simone. Until your 'husband' came on the scene, we were happy, we're even engaged for God's sake! *(He looks at her thoughtfully)* You want us to end, don't you?
SIMONE *(uncertain)* No. Of course not.
ROGER Well, we can't go on can we? I can't trust you now. Our relationship has been rapidly going down the pan these last few months. You're making me out to be a saddo emotional wreck because of my upbringing and now you're throwing it back in my face when it suits you. Thanks, that doesn't make me feel any better *(She tries to interrupt)* No, it's true, don't deny it. Everything that I've told you was because I thought I could trust you. But now I wouldn't trust you to tell me the time. It just feels like you want us to end, because all I seem to do lately is irritate you. And not only that, you never want to go out lately either.
SIMONE Don't blame me for that, you're always complaining that you 'want your space'. All I'm doing is giving it to you.
ROGER *(Scoffing)* Oh that's nice! That is such a cheap cop out Simone. Yes, I like 'my own space' and so do you; but that's not the 'space' I mean. I mean the 'space' you give me when you don't turn up to the theatre when we arranged to go; remember when you begged me to get tickets for you favourite play 'Abigail's Party' at the Octagon Theatre and you stood me up?
SIMONE *(sheepishly)* And I told you what happened; I got stuck on the East Lancs Road coming out of Manchester because of an accident.
ROGER Yeah, you told me. Two days later after I panicked and fretted over if you were hurt or not! Two days after leaving you messages on your answering machine, leaving voice-mail messages on your mobile; god knows how many text messages I sent you and all the frantic phone calls to A and E.
SIMONE You did go a little over the top I thought.
ROGER *(exploding)* Over the top?! I was fucking frantic with worry you stupid cow! How did you expect me to be after not knowing what had happened to you?
SIMONE Nothing happened to me.
ROGER I know that, two days after when I come home from work and find you sat on the settee calmly eating cheese on toast while watching Basic Instinct *and* you wouldn't answer my questions. In fact, you still haven't told me where you were for those two days, and you had the cheek to have a go at me for seeing the play without you!
SIMONE I did think you had a nerve going to see it without me. You know that it's my favourite play.

ROGER I left your ticket at the box office just in case you could have made it, but you didn't. It's totally unbelievable behaviour from you. But now I can guess what you were up to; you were with Mike – shagging him in some seedy hotel in Manchester.
SIMONE *(Hesitantly)* Don't be daft, I got stuck in traffic, that's all. I didn't have my mobile with me, by the time I got home it was eight thirty and I was so exhausted I just went straight to bed. I just didn't think about the play and that's it. I've told you until I'm blue in the face that I was just stressed out and needed a little space. And as soon as I got all your messages I contacted you straight away.
ROGER Have you any idea how pathetic and unbelievable that sounds?
SIMONE It's true. More true than a seedy hotel.

Roger knows she's lying and studies her speculatively. He pulls out of his pocket his mobile phone and looks for something. Finding it he hands Simone the phone. She tentatively takes it, unsure what to do.

ROGER Read that text message - aloud.
SIMONE *(Taking a deep worried breath)* "Rog, I've just seen your car on the multi storey car park on Oxford Road, are you in town? If you are, do you fancy a drink at the Portland? I'll be there till ten if you do. Pete". *(She hands it back to him)* So, a text message from Pete who saw your car in Manchester, big deal.
ROGER You don't get it do you? Read the date of the message. It was the night that you got 'stuck' in traffic, sent at 8.33pm. It was the first time that I let you drive my car because you wanted to get back home early so you could see Abigail's Party at the Octagon. Remember? *(There is an uneasy silence)* It doesn't take a genius to wonder what you were doing. And if you are wondering why I have never mentioned it before it's because I didn't twig what the hell Pete was on about until last week because I completely forgot all about lending you the car as I didn't need it for a week or so. Remember?
SIMONE *(shrugs)* So, you get a text off Pete and you assume that I'm in a seedy hotel. Wow, you have got a pretty good imagination there Roger, what next I wonder; *(taunting)* maybe *I've* been seen getting off in a sex club in Amsterdam.
ROGER *(exploding)* How many times do you have to be told! I didn't do anything when we went to Amsterdam, firstly because I love you and secondly I spent three days stuck in bed through food poisoning! And it was Richard who got off with that woman and no–one else. And there you go

again, throwing something into the argument to distract it away from you. This is another niggely thing you've been doing lately that's been getting on my nerves.
SIMONE *(angrily)* Roger, *you* are getting on *my* nerves, come straight out with what's on your mind.
ROGER Oh, I'll come out with it, just like I did when you didn't turn up at the Octagon; what the hell is going on? I'm not going over what we argued about because that's not getting me anywhere with you. But Pete also saw you in foyer of the Portland all dolled up 'short skirt and legs' he told me. He was going to say hello to you, but stopped himself when he saw 'Mike who you are not shagging' greet you with - as he put it 'a kiss so passionate even he got an erection'.
SIMONE *(snapping)* That's fucking bollocks! If you were really bothered about what I was doing, then why haven't you mentioned it before?
ROGER *(erupting)* I never stop mentioning it! How many times do I ask you what the hell is going on between you and him? How many times do you deny it? Five minutes ago you casually told me that you were married – to him of all people! *(He is really agitated)* We are through! Finished! I don't want to see you again, is that understood?
SIMONE *(Crying)* No Roger, you don't mean that!
ROGER Oh fuck off! Cut out the fake tears, I've had enough. I've had enough of you, your lies, and your still being married. Now I know why you are so reluctant to move in with me, it's because of him. I wouldn't be surprised if the house you live in was in both your names. Well I hope he's come back to claim his half. *(He looks at her with disdain)* I loved you; I've been totally honest with you these last six years. *(He can't think of anything else to say)* Well, I'll get all my stuff out from yours tomorrow, I'll get a van from my brothers rental firm, he owes me a few favours and I'll be out of your life before dinner time. *(He waits for a response and shrugs when he doesn't get one from the sobbing Simone)* So, is this how we end? Is that it? Six years together and it ends in the place that we first met? Remember that science fiction convention? *(no response)* Right, okay, I'll go then. When I've got my things from your house I'll put the key through your letter box. I'll delete your number from my mobile and. . . . God this is so shitty. . . . . . Do you still love him? *(she doesn't answer)* I'm going to take that as a yes. *(He turns to go and looks back, she isn't looking at him, she sits at the table, sobbing)* Right then. See you. *(Exits)*

After a moment she looks up, breaths a deep sigh of relief. Pulls her mobile phone from her handbag and dials a number, after a moment it answers.

SIMONE Hi Mike, will you come and pick me up? Yes he's gone *finally!* I didn't think he was going to go. Yes I'm where I said we would be - at the Greenery Hotel. How long? Ten minutes? Okay, I'll be in outside waiting for you. Get here as fast as you can. Thanks Mike, bye.

She blows another sigh of relief, lights up a cigarette. Smiles, then smirks.

END

"SHE'S OFF HER FACE(BOOK)"

A lonely man describes how his life has changed in 9 months since he bought his wife a laptop for her birthday and how he isn't impressed with her FACEBOOK addiction.

It is narrated by him as various scenes of the last 9 months are acted out in the form of 'flashbacks'.

And for simplicity the "narrator" is listed as a separate 'character', or it can be played by a different actor as well. Also, apart from Sarah, the other female characters can be played by one actor.

CHARACTERS

KEVIN/NARRATOR	HUSBAND
SARAH	WIFE
ISABELLE	SARAH'S OLD FRIEND
SHARON	SARAH'S OLD FRIEND
LEANNE	A WORK COLLEAGUE

SCENES

SCENE ONE	CINEMA CAR PARK
SCENE TWO	LIVING ROOM
SCENE THREE	LIVING ROOM (nine months later)
SCENE FOUR	BIRTHDAY OFFER
SCENE FIVE	MEETING ISABELLE
SCENE SIX	MEETING SHARON
SCENE SEVEN	KEVIN CRACKS
SCENE EIGHT	KEVIN AND LEANNE
SCENE NINE	ULTIMATUM
SCENE TEN	CASINO

SCENE ONE CINEMA CAR PARK

Kevin and Sarah are happily walking to their car from the cinema.

KEVIN Wow!! What a film! I can see why you like that actor.
SARAH He's so lush and fit! I wish you were him sometimes.
KEVIN Eh, what d'ya mean? What's wrong with me hmm?
SARAH I'd like you to be more macho and a bit rough with me sometimes. You know. . . . in the bedroom.
KEVIN So I'm not macho enough for you then? What would prove my manliness to you? Would you like me to throw you around the bed like he did with that very amply chested woman?
SARAH *(excited)* Ooh, yes please.
KEVIN And would you want me to rip off that tight fitting corset and ravish you, like he did with that very ample bosomed woman?
SARAH Ooh, even better!!
KEVIN I'm getting very turned on just thinking about getting you home and ravishing you.
SARAH I can tell! Now hurry up and get us home. Pity you parked the car so far away, I'm wanting you now.
KEVIN Don't blame me, blame Orange Wednesdays for the full car park.
SARAH *(lustfully)* I can't wait! Let's do it here!
KEVIN Yeah!!
SARAH Blimey Kevin, you're sex mad! You're always randy lately!
KEVIN Don't blame me for my continual randiness, it's your fault you know.
SARAH My fault? How do you work that out?
KEVIN It's you being so insatiable, it turns me on, that's why. *(He nuzzles her neck)*
SARAH *(squealing in delight)* Behave Kevin.
KEVIN And I love your neck, I want to bite it and suck out your blood.
SARAH Ooh, yes please! But don't leave a nasty bruise though.
KEVIN Have I ever?
SARAH Ooh Kevin.........

They kiss passionately as the lights fade.

<u>SCENE TWO</u> LIVING ROOM

They are snuggled up on the settee watching a movie feeding each other sweets.

SARAH *(Dreamily)* I love watching films with you, all snuggled up on the couch holding hands.
KEVIN I do too. I've never got bored with doing this with you, ever.
SARAH Not even after nine years?
KEVIN Not even after nine hundred years.
SARAH Awe, I love you Kevin.
KEVIN I love you too Sarah.
SARAH I hope nothing comes between us and we're happily married till we're old and grey. Well, me old and grey, you wrinkly and bald.
KEVIN I could wear a wig.
SARAH Awe, you never take me on when I insult your balding head do you?
KEVIN What's the point? It doesn't insult me because baldness is a sign of virility isn't it. And I'm certainly that.
SARAH Pity you can't get me pregnant though.
KEVIN Not for want of trying. And I enjoy the trying.
SARAH You find sex with me 'trying'?
KEVIN Nooo, don't be silly. It's a phrase what people say ain't it? When a married couple want a child they call it 'trying for a baby'. Which always makes me laugh. Why don't they just say they're screwing every moment they can?
SARAH *(giggles)* Like us in the car park last Wednesday.
KEVIN Oh yeah.
SARAH Yeah, but there's more to making a baby than screwing every moment we can you know. It's very scientific.
KEVIN Eh? What are you on about?
SARAH Well, there's knowing when in my cycle I'm ovulating. Taking temperatures so I know exactly when it's happening and then getting the man in to put the finishing touch to it with his weapon of impregnation.
KEVIN *(Teasing)* That's all very well for you you know, you make me sound like the sperminator or something. What if at the time of your ovulation I've got a headache?
SARAH You better not have one when the time happens or. . . .
KEVIN Or what? Wouldn't a turkey baster do the job more efficiently?
SARAH You cheeky git!

KEVIN Ha ha, gotcha!! *(he tickles Sarah and she squeals with happiness)* Awe, we're out of Malteasers. Have we got another box?
SARAH We've got 4. I made sure we were well stocked up for tonight.
KEVIN *(kisses her)* And that's why I love you, because you're so organised. *(he stands up)* don't go away will you?
SARAH *(sexily)* I'll be right here sweety. And bring in another bottle of wine while you're in the kitchen. It's chilling in the fridge.
KEVIN *(salutes)* Aye aye captain.

LIGHTS FADE

SPOTLIGHT

Kevin is now The Narrator

NARRATOR Sarah and I have been married for nine years, we had been going out with each other for six months before we realised that we had a very special connection and that nothing else in the world mattered except being together for the rest of our lives. So one day we just decided to get married on the spur of the moment. No engagement ring, no party for family who can't stand each other. Just me, Sarah, her best friend Isabelle as witness and the fee to the registrar who we bribed to take a few photo's of the event. Obviously when our family found out there was a mixed reaction, but mainly it was a positive one. I loved her then and I love her now. She's my soul mate.

We never argue, we never fight. We still make love five, sometimes six times a week. I like the house we live in that we both love and chose together. We have a dog called Brandy, after our favourite drink, and cat, named Shandy. Also a rabbit and a guinea pig. The perfect 'family'. Except that we don't have any children. Not that we haven't 'tried' for them. That's always great and we do still have a healthy sexual appetite and we haven't had any extra marital affairs, nobody else comes close to what we like or want in a person and we've never even thought about it. We have no reason to stray and if we did, the guilt would be unbearable.

At the moment we are both in extremely well paid jobs, but it's looking like Sarah's company is moving abroad and she isn't part of the plans for redeployment, so after 15 years she's been offered a very generous severance payment that will keep us afloat for a couple of years should I fall into the 'redundant' category as well. We share the same interests, but I do like to have a good night at the casino now and again, something Sarah can't abide, but on those nights she has her friends round for a girlie night while I sometimes blow up to £200 each and every night I go. We like the cinema, sometime we go 3 times a week. I watch a film she wants to see and vica versa and one film that we just chose on the night. And we definitely do not have a computer. The only technology we have is the latest 4g phone, a DVD recorder *and* a 48 inch flat screen TV, plus the best all round stereo system since Dolby was invented, but that's about it. Though lately she has been dropping big hints for me to get her one of those sky packages for her birthday. You know the ones, free view box with a million channels, free phone calls all weekends and evenings and broadband internet connection. All for £15 a month. The trouble is; she's going to need a computer and she's been dropping big hints for not only the sky package, but also for a laptop computer to go with it. And you know what? I might just buy one for her. I personally don't want to buy her one, but what the heck eh? What harm can it do? The only problem is asking her when the time is right. Fast forward nine months and this what our evenings are like.

SPOTLIGHT off.

SCENE THREE LIVING ROOM *(nine months later)*

The television is on, the volume is loud, but they aren't taking much notice of it. Sarah is hunched over a laptop computer laughing to herself, at the side of her seat there are crisp packets and a big bottle of coke. Kevin is fed up and drinking a bottle of beer and huffing while looking through the Argos catalogue. He rises and looks around the room for something.

KEVIN Have you seen the remote? *(he waits for a reply, none is forthcoming. He sighs)* Have you seen the remote? *(He kicks her foot)*
SARAH *(doesn't look up)* Ow!! What do you want?
KEVIN Have you seen the remote control for the telly?
SARAH *(grunts)* I dunno where it is.
KEVIN Will you help me look for it please?
SARAH Why?
KEVIN Because I want to change the channel that's why.
SARAH I'll look for it later, give me a minute, let me finish this game.
KEVIN *(Annoyed, childish voice)* Let me finish this game. You're always on that damn PC, I wish I never bought it for you.

SARAH *(Doesn't look up)* Oh shut up and make me a brew.

Kevin is resigned to his fate for the evening. He turns to face the audience.

SPOTLIGHT

NARRATOR This what our life is like now since she was 'let go' by her company. She didn't get the big payoff they promised her and she's got pretty depressed over it. Which is understandable. All we do is stay in every night and she is on her damn laptop nearly all day. The only time she isn't on it is when she goes to the toilet or falls asleep at two in the morning after being on it all day from the moment she wakes up around nine o'clock or so. Ten if she fancies a 'lie-in'. And it's all my fault that we are like this and I can't see a way out of it. I've tried everything to distract her, but she doesn't take me on. I've basically lost her. I hate computers. I hate what they have done to our marriage. Don't get me wrong, I can work my way around them, go 'online' and 'surf the web' and all that; but I hate what they have done to my marriage. Yep, as you saw earlier, nine months ago we were a normal hard working happily married couple, until the day I uttered the immortal words to my wife.

SPOTLIGHT OFF

SCENE FOUR BIRTHDAY OFFER

KEVIN What would you like for your birthday?
SARAH I haven't given it a thought. How much are you going to spend on me?
KEVIN A tenner?
SARAH Ha ha. I don't think so, I'm worth more than a tenner.
KEVIN Well, you've always been going on about getting that sky TV/broadband/phone package, what about that?
SARAH Did I ask for that? I might have been joking you know.
KEVIN You sure did. How about it? Do you want it?
SARAH It's a bit bland isn't it. How about a nice pair of shoes?
KEVIN Shoes? You've got about 3 million pairs of shoes upstairs as it is. Nope, sorry, no shoes.
SARAH Aww!! You're being stingy!
KEVIN No I'm not. Anyway, it was only last night you were complaining about nothing on the telly and all the good stuff was on Sky. So?

SARAH So? Just a broadband package? What else?
KEVIN I'll throw in a laptop computer, what do you say to that? I've seen some good ones in the Argos catalogue for about £300.
SARAH Nah, how about a weekend in Paris?
KEVIN No chance!! Here, have a look at them and see what you think. It's either that or a cheapo ring from Half Price Jewellers.
SARAH Oh go on then if you insist. I can't see the point of them really. 'Online shopping', 'google'. What's it all about eh? People shopping on line is the weird thing. What's wrong with actual 'shopping'? You know, being stuck in a queue behind someone who's forgotten their Pin number ect ect.
KEVIN You hate shopping in shops!! You're the only woman I know that doesn't like going round Manchester on a Saturday, that's one of the reasons why I fell in love with you in the first place.
SARAH Oh go on then. Give it here and let me have a look.

He passes over the Argos catalogue.

SPOTLIGHT

NARRATOR And that was how it began. Sarah chose a laptop for £350 that came with a printer and in the end we got a BT online package, phone, broadband and TV and for the first month it hardly got touched and I was getting very annoyed with her, saying that I had wasted all that money and that we should have gone to Paris after all. But one night while we were cuddled up on the couch watching Starship Troopers with a bottle of bubbly on ice, an advert came on. About shoes. Sarah has a thing for shoes that I've never understood, just like she doesn't understand why I go to the casino I suppose. And at the end of it the voice over guy said 'for details of our range "go online". Well that was it. She did. That night. For SEVEN HOURS!! The bottle of bubbly went warm when the ice melted and the delivered Chinese that I ordered I ate myself. But much worse was to come.

SPOTLIGHT off

SCENE FIVE MEETING ISABELLE

Sarah is walking down the street. Her friend Isabelle is walking towards her and they are excited to see each other.

SARAH Isabelle!! Nice to see you, wow, how long has it been?

They hug.

ISABELLE Blimey, four years isn't it?
SARAH Wow, that long? How's it going in Stockport with the new hubby? What's this one? Number three isn't he?
ISABELLE Number three went ages ago, I'm on number four now.
SARAH *(Shocked)* Number four? I thought you was happy with Michael.
ISABELLE I was, until he ran out of money and couldn't support me. He said he was a millionaire, it turns out he was living on hundred grand overdraft. He had to sell the house we lived in for £60,000 less than market value just to pay me off. It was a struggle I can tell you.
SARAH I bet it was. So how's it going with hubby number four? Thanks for inviting us to the wedding by the way.
ISABELLE Not bad, not bad. He's a dream. Stockport's a dump, I'm nagging him to move, I've seen this great house in Wilmslow but he won't budge. Sorry about not inviting you, I didn't know if you could make it. We stayed in a really exquisite country hotel! Nearly two hundred pounds a night! For three weeks. Ooh it was lovely. Anyway, how's you and Kelvin?
SARAH *(annoyed)* Kevin. His name is Kevin. *(brightly)* Yeah, we're doing great. Nine years now.
ISABELLE *(amazed)* Nine years eh? Where does the time go?
SARAH I know!! Anyway, you witnessed me getting married, remember?
ISABELLE How could I forget? I thought you were mad.
SARAH Mad? Why?
ISABELLE Well you were mad to get married so soon after meeting him *and* getting married in a registrar office as well. I would have held out for a big lavish wedding me.
SARAH *(irritated)* Yes, how is your new marriage coming along?
ISABELLE Great! He's loaded!
SARAH *(sarcastic)* Once again, thanks for the invite.
ISABELLE *(puzzled)* Did I invite you? I don't remember receiving a present from you.
SARAH *(annoyed)* You didn't invite us that's why you didn't get a present!
ISABELLE I can't think why I didn't invite you. Oh well, I'm sorry *(she hugs Sarah)* How many kids have you got?
SARAH None. Yet.
ISABELLE No kids? Why? Is he firing blanks?

SARAH Quite possibly. It's okay, I've got used to the idea of having no kids. We've got a dog and cat, plus a Guinea Pig and a rabbit, so they're a handful anyway. Plus Kevin as well *(laughs)*
ISABELLE *(puzzled)* A rabbit? The battery kind rampant ones?
SARAH *(sighing)* No, just a normal one that eats leaves and runs around the garden type.
ISABELLE That's boring! And a dog you say? I'd love a dog, but my fella won't entertain it. You should have a couple of little kids running around by now Sarah, your biological clock is ticking and you'll regret not having any you know. Kids make a marriage, they make it complete you know.
SARAH I know, but what can I do? We've tried everything. I might go for a sperm donor and see how that goes. Have you got any kids Isabelle?
ISABELLE *(Scornfully)* You're joking! I don't want kids! Little rug rats running around the house spending your money. Stuff that for a game of soldiers!
SARAH *(Confused)* If you don't want kids then why did you ask me if I have any?
ISABELLE *(looks at her expensive watch)* Look, I'm not being rude, but I'm already late for my hair appointment.
SARAH *(stunned at the quick change of subject)* Hair appointment? You've travelled all the way from Stockport to have your hair done?
ISABELLE It's a friend of my sister, she's a student or whatever they call them people who do hair. She's doing my hair for her final exam for her NVQ and I'm not one to pass up a freebie as you know.
SARAH *(Muttering)* How could I forget?
ISABELLE *(Air kisses)* Look, we must catch up. Look out for me on Facebook. All my wedding photos are on my page, so you'll see what you missed. Add me. *(she walks off)*

SPOTLIGHT

NARRATOR Those fatal words "Look me up on Facebook", then "Add me". After that, life for both of us changed forever.

SPOTLIGHT off

Sarah enters the room and picks up the laptop. Kevin is watching the TV

SARAH Hi love, have you had a good day?
KEVIN I certainly have. I won £90 on the horses today.

SARAH Ooh lovely. So a Chinese takeout for supper then?
KEVIN Certainly my dear. How about a banquet?
SARAH Ooh, yes please. *(she is engrossed on the PC now)*
KEVIN *(shocked)* Wow, what's going on? You've not bothered to touch that for weeks and now you're using it. Don't tell me, you need new shoes.
SARAH Nope, wrong. Have you ever heard of Facebook?
KEVIN *(Groans)* Oh no, you don't want to go on that do you? It's evil, it takes away your life.
SARAH Don't be silly, how can something like that take over your life?
KEVIN Believe me, it does. That's all the guys at work ever talk about. You'll never go out again. It's very addictive.
SARAH Well it won't get me addicted.
KEVIN You wanna bet? Anyway, what's brought this on?
SARAH I bumped into Isabelle Waring today and. . . .
KEVIN Whoa. Isabelle? Isabelle the one with the big *(indicates chest)*
SARAH *(looking up, annoyed)* Yes, that Isabelle.
KEVIN The same Isabelle who invited us to one of her weddings?
SARAH The very same. But get this; she's on her fourth husband now.
KEVIN *(surprised)* Her fourth? Why didn't we get invited?
SARAH She was too busy spending his money! And she gave me some advice about how not being a parent is running down my 'biological clock'. As if she can talk.
KEVIN I heard she lives in Stockport. What's she doing here? You didn't you go to Stockport did you?
SARAH No, anyway, you wouldn't let me use the car, remember? No, she was back in town for a free haircut. You know what a free loader she is.
KEVIN I sure do, she still has my James Herbert books, did you mention that to her?
SARAH Don't be daft. I don't even know why you lent them to her. Or where you trying to impress?
KEVIN Impress? What do you mean?
SARAH It doesn't matter. Anyway, you might as well write them off as she'll have forgotten about them and give them to a charity shop knowing her. Come to think of it, she wouldn't know what a charity shop is!
KEVIN She better not have, they're all first edition hardbacks. So you met the leach then?
SARAH Don't call her that!!
KEVIN Okay I won't. *(under his breath)* Leach! So what did she have to say for herself?
SARAH She wants to move to Wilmslow but her chap won't budge.

KEVIN Ah, I see. So you're looking at houses in Wilmslow are you? You want to move so you can be with her, that's it isn't it?
SARAH No, don't be daft!! She said find her on Facebook and add her. I've never heard of Facebook.
KEVIN And like I said, you don't want to.
SARAH Why?
KEVIN Because it's evil, you'll never leave the house again because you'll be playing silly game and all the shit that goes with it.
SARAH A-ha! Found it. "Facebook is a social utility site that connects friends. . . . "
KEVIN *(Interrupting)* You don't want to go on it, listen to me.
SARAH Oh.
KEVIN What?
SARAH I don't have an email address.
KEVIN *(smug)* Awe, what a shame. You can't go on it then can you?
SARAH Oh bugger!!
KEVIN What?
SARAH The screens gone blank. There's no power. Damn, the fuse has gone! Bleeding cheapo PC! I wish you had taken me to Paris now. Bloody damn crappy thing!

SPOTLIGHT

NARRATOR Yes, but the fuse hadn't gone. The screen had broken and the the damn thing was too expensive to repair. Well, that's what I told her anyway. But it didn't stop her – oh no. She went to the library and registered an email address from there and while she was in the library she bumped into Sharon, who, as it turned out, was a Facebook 'expert' of 3 years.

SPOTLIGHT off

SCENE SIX MEETING SHARON

SHARON Hi!! I thought it was you!! What are doing in a library?
SARAH *(stunned)* Sharon?! Hi! Nice to see you. My laptop has broken and I'm signing up for an email address.
SHARON Oh? What for?
SARAH I need one so I can go on Facebook.
SHARON I'm on Facebook, it's great! I've met loads of friends from school on that, it's fab.

SARAH Fab? I didn't know people still used that word.
SHARON Okay, it's ace. It's about time you joined the twentieth century.
SARAH I'm glad you think so. Kevin thinks it's the work of the devil.
SHARON *(dismissive)* Phaw, what does he know?
SARAH If it isn't a horse or the casino, nothing much. There, done it. I now have an email address.
SHARON Right, now all you need to do is go register and away we go.
SARAH How long have you been on Facebook then?
SHARON Three years now, it's a laugh, there's loads of games to play and Mafia Wars.
SARAH Mafia Wars? What's that?
SHARON I'll show you when you go on. It's dead good.
SARAH Wow, it wants a lot of info off me doesn't it?
SHARON You can fill all that in later. Add me.
SARAH How do I do that?
SHARON In the top right hand corner there is a box. Type my name in and press return. It searches out people with that name and you find the one you want. Type 'Sharon Halestead', press return. There, you've found me.
SARAH Which one are you? There's 498 Sharon Halesteads.
SHARON I'm there, right at the top.
SARAH What are you wearing?
SHARON *(Laughs)* It's a bin bag and Scooby Doo mask I was wearing for a fancy dress party.
SARAH Why?
SHARON I was pissed, I can't remember why *(she takes out her mobile phone)* Press 'add as friend'. Okay, it'll notify me that you've put a friend request to me. There, done. You're now my Facebook friend.
SARAH How have you done that?
SHARON I've got it on my phone. I'm your first friend on Facebook, now you just need some more and you're off.
SARAH Wow, you've got 600 friends, you don't know all them do you?
SHARON I know about hundred, the rest are my Mafia Wars friends. Check out my friends list, you might know some of them from school. I've got to go now, work calls. I'll send you some games and I'll message you later. See you later on Facebook.

SPOTLIGHT

NARRATOR And with that Sarah was hooked. Within one week she had fifty friends and there was many nights she'd be giggling over something she had sent to her for her "Super Fun Wall" and she would be chatting 'online' to someone from her old school or college or work who I hadn't heard of. Even our milkman was her "Facebook Friend". Her friends list quickly expanded to 200 in a month and she would be playing "Vampire Wars" or Bejewelled Blitz" until one in the morning. I very quickly got ignored. So much that I even learned to use the cooker and make my own meals. I've become quite a chef in the kitchen now. Things got very strained between us, especially when she bought a new Laptop and an I-Phone that she played with while we were on the train to Glasgow. That was quite a strained journey I can tell you. Facebook. It took over her life. Totally.

SPOTLIGHT OFF

SARAH Look Kevin you just don't get it do you? Facebook is great! I get to look at people's pages and find out what they are doing with their status updates. I've met up with old friends I haven't seen in years and we chat all the time. Plus all the games and people writing on my wall and me theirs. It's fun, you should come on it, it's just *fun* that's all.

SPOTLIGHT ON

KEVIN For her it became a "voyeurs heaven". And as she said, she found out so much about her friends by looking at their pages and status updates and she quickly became a regular viewer – or nosey as I call it. She was reunited with friends she hadn't seen in years and chatted 'online' with them for hours and many evenings she would be sat in her chair with a bottle of wine, or whisky, or vodka or whatever alcohol we had in the house while eating huge packets of Doritito's and wrote on walls while throwing pigs at her friends and sending hearts and playing those stupid pointless quizzes! Oh, did I say that I got very pissed off with her? I feel like I'm repeating myself and talking to myself and repeating myself and talking to myself sometimes. *(pause)* God, I'm so depressed.

SPOTLIGHT off

SCENE SEVEN KEVIN CRACKS

KEVIN The dog needs walking. Do want to come with me? It's a nice night, go for a nice walk, get fit, have a chat. Pop into the pub for a drink or two. What do you say? Fancy it?

SARAH *(Not looking up from screen)* No thanks.
KEVIN You and this sodding Facebook!! What the hell can you do on it for five bleeding hours?
SARAH I'm talking to my friend Shirley.

Kevin snaps. He tries to take the laptop off her, but her grip is strong.

Get off!! What you doing?
KEVIN *(firmly)* I want you to turn that off and come for a walk with me and Brandy. Please.
SARAH *(yelling)* Nooo okay! Just go alright. Walk the stupid mutt.
KEVIN How the heck have you got 756 friends? You don't know that many people. Apart from work, your mates and a few of mine, you only know about twenty people– if that.
SARAH *(petulantly)* They are my Mafia friends. Okay Columbo.
KEVIN Mafia? What are you going on about? And who are you talking to? Colin? Whose Colin? That's not Shirley! Who the hell is that guy?.

She angrily snaps shut the laptop and sulks.

SARAH Go away!! Stop being so nosey. Go and walk Brandy and leave me alone.
KEVIN Nosey?! I'm your husband! I think I have a right to know who my wife is talking to 'online'. Who is this Colin? How do you know him?
SARAH He's in my Mafia Wars. His name is "La Don Col". He helped me round up the drug lords. We were just chatting about tactics and stuff.
KEVIN *(Dismissive)* Yeah, right. Have you met him?
SARAH No!! He lives in California for god's sake! So there's no chance of that is there!!
KEVIN Phah, California my arse! He should live in Chicago, then you're stupid Mafia colleague would be more believable! I'm going out.
SARAH Where you going?
KEVIN To the pub. See you tomorrow, when I get back I'm going to sleep in the spare room.
SARAH What about the dog? Aren't you taking her for a walk?
KEVIN No. Tie her up in the back yard and let her howl all night like I do when see you on that bloody laptop!!

SPOTLIGHT

NARRATOR Mafia Wars. She was bored one night and logged on to the laptop and got sent 'energy packs' from her brother and his friends who asked her to join their Mafia family, so she did because 'she was needed in their fight to bring down the evil Don'. So she enrolled and became "Don Sarah the Ker", a mogul, so she could earn money fast. And that was at eight o'clock. She was hooked and was still playing at two in the morning. At first she had a very small Mafia and her advancement was very slow because she only received 'energy packs' off her Mafia family every 24 hours and she would be up till three some nights playing the dam thing. So, to speed things up, she joined a 'pimping site' and soon got a very large Mafia family by befriending people from all over the world and that's how her friends list grew. You would have thought she would leave it there, but oh no – she became an 'aficionado' and gave all her new found friends gifts on their 'wish list' that they required. She said to me that she felt 'connected with her facebook friends and wasn't lonely anymore'. Make of that what you will.

Anyway, not to be disheartened I went out most nights and left her to it. She never noticed me coming home because she had flaked out in front of the telly, laptop clutched tightly to her chest in the likely event that I would have a mooch at what she was up to. I couldn't care less. I joined a gym and went to the cinema on my own. It felt strange, but I soon got used to it. Then at work we had a new member of staff joining us from our London office. Leanne. 23, Gorgeous, sexy, smart. Too good for me, she was well out of my league. Or so I thought. Somehow we ended up working together and now and again we would go for a drink after work and I honestly thought my moaning and talking about my wife would put her off me. How wrong could I be?

SPOTLIGHT off

SCENE EIGHT <u>KEVIN AND LEANNE</u>

KEVIN Awe, I wish I had seen that, it sounds like a good film.
LEANNE It is, in fact it's on DVD, you should rent it and watch it with Sarah, you'll love it. Anyway, I didn't know you were into 'girly films. I thought Bruce Willis was more your type of movie.
KEVIN Phh, don't mention Sarah, she doesn't even know I exist anymore since she went on 'Facebook'.

LEANNE *(Scornfully)* Facebook? Don't talk to me about that shit. I was on it for two years, it ended my relationship with Simon because I never went out for months because I was on it all the time. In the end he dumped me with the classic line "stop poking my friends and playing those stupid games! It's either that or me". Guess what I chose?
KEVIN Facebook.
LEANNE Got it in one. And you know, when he finished with me I wasn't bothered, but looking back on it I can see where he was coming from.
KEVIN Well the way things are going between me and Sarah I can see us getting a divorce.
LEANNE Oh no honey, that's a bit drastic isn't it?
KEVIN You think so? She's on it from morning till night. There's been lots of times I've gone to bed leaving her to play her stupid Mafia Wars and got up in the morning to find her asleep in her chair with her laptop sliding off her. She's never been the same since she lost her job, it's all she's living for.
LEANNE (*sympathetically*) Oh no, that's not good is it?
KEVIN I just can't see what she sees in it.
LEANNE You've become a "facebook widower".
KEVIN I wouldn't go *that* far. Actually, yes I would *(laughs)* I wouldn't mind, but it was my idea to get her a damn laptop, TV and broadband package for her birthday in the first place. I should have took her to Paris like she dropped big hints for. I feel neglected and my "needs" are being ignored. It was never like this before I bought her that damn laptop
LEANNE *(stroking his leg)* Aww my poor Kevin.
KEVIN Aww, poor me indeed.
LEANNE So what are you doing while she's wasting her life away?
KEVIN Oh, you know, walking the dog a lot .. . . I've joined a gym. . . . I've lost 2 stone.
LEANNE Hey, good for you. I thought you looked trimmer when I saw you last week.
KEVIN Thank you Leanne, I'm glad you've noticed. Unlike Sarah.
LEANNE *(her hand rising further up his leg)* Which gym have you joined?
KEVIN Total Fitness.
LEANNE I go there, I joined a few weeks ago. Maybe we could work out sometime?
KEVIN Yeah, you're on.
LEANNE *(suggestively)* I must warn you that I train hard. And fast.
KEVIN *(knowing what she means)* That's just how I like it too.
LEANNE Thanks for asking me out for a drink tonight.
KEVIN My pleasure, thanks for coming.

LEANNE *(suggestively)* No problem, I wanted to *come*. With you. Maybe I could help you out with your "needs". I have "needs" too you know.

The chat is becoming more and more suggestive. They move to kiss each other.

SPOTLIGHT

NARRATOR And that is how my 8 week shag fest with Leanne started and I loved every second of it, until the day she became "Facebook friends" with Sarah. That stopped everything between us stone dead.

SPOTLIGHT off

KEVIN *(angrily)* What do you think you were doing?
LEANNE Oh don't be so paranoid.
KEVIN Becoming friends with Sarah on Facebook? Are you nuts? She's asked me loads of questions about you and I told her that I know you only from work. If she knew that we were shagging each other. . . . !
LEANNE *(laughing)* Don't be stupid Kevin. I wouldn't tell her anyway.
KEVIN Yeah? How do I know?
LEANNE She already knows about us anyway doesn't she? Remember? You told her that we go to the gym together and she was okay with that you said.
KEVIN She was fine with it until she saw your picture and how gorgeous and toned you are. She feels a frump compared to you and she's been asking questions ever since. Have you chatted 'online'?
LEANNE No, she's just added me as her friend because we are both in Mafia wars. We have a few mutual friends that's all. I didn't mean to put a friend request to her, I was a bit drunk that night and so were you if I remember.
KEVIN Drunk? If I remember rightly the night you put your 'friend request' to Sarah was the night you blew me off and didn't go to the gym. Why was that? So you could stare things up between us?
LEANNE Us?
KEVIN Sarah and me.
LEANNE No. I told you I was drunk, I didn't mean it. I'm sorry.
KEVIN I can't believe that you blew me off for a night on Facebook!
LEANNE I didn't. I got home late from work like I told you and I was tired and a bit bored. . . .

KEVIN Bored? I wanted to come round. I wanted us to go to the gym. You wouldn't have been bored if I had come round would you.
LEANNE *(looks him straight in the eye, firmly)* Maybe I didn't want to you to come round.
KEVIN *(shocked)* What?
LEANNE Maybe I didn't want you to come round.
KEVIN Why? Don't you like me coming round?
LEANNE Yes, but maybe you've been coming round too often.
KEVIN What do you mean? Are you bored with me?
LEANNE *(Awkwardly)* No, the sex is fucking fantastic and for a man of your age to do it 3 times a night is amazing, but. . . .
KEVIN What do you mean 'a man of my age'? I'm only 39 you know!
LEANNE Look, Kevin, I really like you, I do. But I don't think it's right that you are married and. . .
KEVIN What? That we are having sex? Is that it? I don't see anything wrong with it.
LEANNE Well, maybe that's the problem.
Kevin is saddened and annoyed. His 'escape' from his wife has gone.

LEANNE I'm sorry. We could still be friends and go to the gym together.
KEVIN *(Sadly)* No, I don't think so. So, this is it then? Goodbye? (*He suddenly hugs her and they kiss passionately.)*
LEANNE *(breaking away, gets her breath back)* Wow! I'll miss you. And don't worry, I won't grass you up to you wife.

SPOTLIGHT

NARRATOR And with that she was out of my life as soon as she entered it. I'll give her her due, so far she hasn't mentioned us and at work she avoids me like a plague and she's cancelled her gym membership. But hey, I don't regret any of it. She was - a great girl. I bet you thought I was going to say a 'great fuck' didn't you? Well, she was, and she thought I was too. But I never told her I was taking Viagra, but hey, when a woman is as beautiful as she is, you don't want to disappoint her and it all be over in 2 minutes do you?

Anyway, that night I went to the gym for a work out. I took out my anger on the cross trainer. I did an hour, which is amazing because I've never managed more than 35 minutes. And then I went to Leanne's and mines favourite pub and got totally pissed. Somehow I got home and I had the horniest dream that Sarah and I were making love like the good old days. It felt so real, like she was in the bed with me. But when I finally woke up the next morning my bed was empty. I had fallen out of it.

SPOTLIGHT off

SCENE NINE ULTIMATUM

KEVIN *(looking through the paper)* Do you fancy going to the pictures?
SARAH *(not really listening)* I've already been.
KEVIN Eh? What are you going on about? I asked you if you fancy going to the pictures tonight.
SARAH *(vaguely interested)*What's on?
KEVIN Well, there's a film starring your favourite actor, that one you mithered me to see when you knew he was going to be in it.
SARAH No thanks. I read a review on Facebook that said it was too long, corny and crap.
KEVIN One review doesn't make it rubbish you know. Come on, let's go. My treat.
SARAH Not tonight, I want to finish working on my farm.
KEVIN Farm? What farm? Since when did you have an interest in farming? You can't stand pigs and cows.
SARAH Not a real farm, my facebook farm. I only need to collect all the grain and send it to market and I earn 3000 points. I'm ahead of ISABELLE by 4000 points already, if I get it done tonight I'm well in front. I've nearly reached top level.
KEVIN You're mad you know that don't you.
SARAH You go, I'm not in the mood.
KEVIN Go to the cinema on my own? I'll get stared at.
SARAH And don't come home too late like you did on Monday night.
KEVIN I came home at midnight, that's not late.
SARAH It is. And don't make any noise either, you woke me up.
KEVIN It's not my fault that you chose that night to go to bed early is it? Unbelievable! Leanne was right, I am a "facebook widower".
SARAH Oh yeah, Leanne, that "bird" you said you were "shagging".
KEVIN *(coolly)* I was only "shagging" her because you are too bothered about that bloody facebook and ignore my obvious need for some physical attention from my wife.
SARAH Whatever Trevor. Anyway, she wouldn't touch you with a barge pole, so don't tell lies will you? You're lips move when you do.
KEVIN Ha ha. Not funny. So you don't want to see a film then?

SARAH No, just go out and leave me alone okay.
KEVIN Okay I will. So you wouldn't mind if I go to a massage parlour on the way home then?
SARAH Do what you want, but get a bottle of milk on your way home and don't forget to walk Brandy.
KEVIN Milk? Walk the dog? Why didn't you get milk when you did the big shop yesterday?
SARAH I forgot. Sorry.
KEVIN You forgot? How could you forget? We have milk with everything, it's the most essential thing we use, for brews, breakfast cereal, your mugs of horlicks that you've been drinking lately. Anything else you 'forget'? Did you forget to pay the O2 bill for your dam interweb broadband facebook connection? Oh, sorry, I forgot; that goes out by direct debit out of *my* bank account. You're going too far with that bleeding arsebook, it's taken over your life. I'm going out and I might stay out late, you know, go to the casino and meet real people. I might send you a message via facebook, at least that way you will notice me and that I exist! And you walk the dog, get some of that wobbly fat off your gut, it'll do you some good going out into the *real* world. And while you're at it, get some milk!

He angrily storms out of the living room. After a moment Sarah looks up.

SARAH Don't get that green top stuff, it's horrible. *(Notices he's not there)* Oh, he's not here. Oh well, time to harvest my grain and milk the cows. *(She busies herself on the laptop)*

SCENE TEN CASINO

Kevin is doing well on the roulette table

SPOTLIGHT

KEVIN A good night tonight, so far I've won £500 and I only came in with £40 so I'm quitting while I'm ahead. The house won't like it, but tough, I've lost enough money in this place. I'm disappointed that Sarah hasn't contacted me. But that's normal now, I'm getting used to it. I just hope she got off her fat arse and got some milk. But I doubt it. I'm getting to the point in which I could easily leave her and she wouldn't notice I've gone. Maybe I should go on facebook and join her Mafia Wars. But would she accept me, that is the question. I can then see what the hell is so exciting about it. Play games, poking people, work on the farm, have loads of lovely ladies as my 'friends', especially Leanne. That would piss Sarah off, probably piss Leanne off as well. In fact, I don't know why I don't just log on to her page and have a mooch. She never logs off, well, if she did I know her password, it's my name, how easy is that?

SPOTLIGHT off

Kevin enters the living room and notices there is no Sarah, the laptop is on the coffee table.

KEVIN Woah, what's going on? *(shouts)* Sarah? Sarah? Well, this is a first *(checks the laptop)* Turned off. Wow! I think now is the time that I had a go on this damn thing! Since I bought it I've not had a sniff. If I went anywhere near it she would almost bite my hand off. Now, let's see what's so dam fantastic about Facebook!

Sarah enters and is stunned to see him on her laptop.

SARAH *(annoyed)* What are you doing on my laptop?!

Kevin is embarrassed, he's caught red handed, banged to rights.

KEVIN I was just, you know, looking at porn, y'know.
SARAH A likely story. You were going to go onto my Facebook page weren't you?
KEVIN *(innocently)* Ooh, er, no, not at all. I was going to log onto that porn site – er, Red Tube.
SARAH No you weren't. I've told you before, when you lie your lips move. Anyway, you can't log onto the laptop because I've changed the password, so there *(pulls out tongue)*
KEVIN *(Unsure how he should approach his question)* Er, where have you been?
SARAH I've been to the park walking Brandy and I've also got us our supper.
KEVIN *(stunned)* Wow, what's brought this on?
SARAH Nothing. I just fancied taking her out for a walk that's all. Got a problem with that?

KEVIN No. And don't be so defensive, blimey. I just asked you where you've been that's all. I've got used to you hunched over your laptop every time I come home from work that's all.
SARAH I'm okay, I just fancied a break from it that's all.
KEVIN *(Stunned)* Pardon? Am I hearing you right?
SARAH There's no need to be Sarcastic you know.
KEVIN I wasn't being sarcastic! I'm stunned that's all. Wow, what's brought this on?
SARAH Nothing, I just got sick of the dog hinting to go for a walk and I just thought – 'sod it'. I put her lead on and I've been out for two hours. Quite liberating really.
KEVIN Two hours isn't much though is it? You waste longer than that writing on walls.
SARAH Yep, you're right. I've been thinking it's crap for quite a while now.
KEVIN *(carefully)* It's not crap. It keeps you in contact with your friends. You love it really.
SARAH It's okay. I just think that it's getting boring now.

Kevin is heartened by what she has just said. There is a glimmer of hope in their marriage after all.

KEVIN Aww, what a shame. I was thinking of signing up as well.
SARAH Don't bother. It takes over your life. I can't believe how many nights I've wasted on it. I might have a mooch later. Anyway, let's enjoy our supper and this bottle of cherry wine I've got you.
KEVIN *(stunned)* Wow, I like cherry wine. Er, I've borrowed Madagascar off my sis. I was expecting a night being by myself as usual, but, er, well. Er. Would you like to watch it with me?
SARAH I love that film! Where you going to watch it on your own?
KEVIN I was actually.
SARAH I don't blame you. I'm sorry.
KEVIN For what?
SARAH For me being so selfish by going on facebook and ignoring you. No wonder you wanted to watch it on your own.
KEVIN It's okay, I understand.
SARAH No it's not okay. I've been extremely selfish to you. I've ignored you and that's not fair is it?
KEVIN It wasn't a problem, honestly. I enjoyed the quiet nights walking the dog, watching telly, going to the gym, pub, snooker, cinema on my own. In

fact, I say you should log on after we've had our supper and watched Madagascar so I can have a nap. What do you say to that?
SARAH *(smiles)* Cheeky git!! *(she kisses him)* You hate me going on Facebook don't you? Lately I've only been going on it just to piss you off and annoy you.
KEVIN What do you mean? You've been going on it just to wind me up?
SARAH Well, to be honest, I've only been going on it when you're home, through the day I've been surfing the web and filling in online job application forms. If I'm really honest. . . . . I've been bored with you.
KEVIN Bored? With me? I don't understand.
SARAH I don't know, I've been wandering around the house like a lost sheep most days and I've been down and very fed up the last few months. What with losing my job and not being able to sign on. I sometimes thank you for buying me the laptop and getting us the Sky telly and broadband. It filled a void for a short time. But a few days ago I woke up and realised that I haven't got a clue what's happening in the world and the fact that I've not seen a film at the cinema with you for ages. And also the fact that you always look worried when you see that I'm logged on. It's like you think I've joined a secret cult or something and I've been brainwashed.

She looks at him with worried expression, but he only has concern and relief coursing through him.

KEVIN I've never thought that at all.
SARAH *(slaps him)* Don't lie.
KEVIN Why? Because my lips move?
SARAH No, because your face tells me everything I need to know. *(she hugs him)* I'm sorry. I'm so sorry. *(she breaks down and cries)*
KEVIN Hey, don't worry. I'm here for you okay. Sssh. Look, facebook is great. It's kept you in touch with your friends and it's been a laugh for you these last 9 months or so. You can still go on it. I don't mind. Just make sure you limit yourself to a couple of hours a day on it and don't go mad. I'm okay with that.
SARAH Don't lie. You've been fed up with me for ages now. I'm surprised you're still talking to me
KEVIN Well, I must admit there have been times when you've tested my patience to the extreme, but I always knew I would get you back. Come here.
SARAH *(Worried)* Why? What are you going to do?
KEVIN Nothing. I'm just going to give you a big hug that's all.

He does so and they kiss. A kiss that says 'forgiveness' from her and 'hello, welcome back' from him.

SARAH Am I forgiven?
KEVIN Well, that depends.
SARAH On what?
KEVIN If you promise to put that damn laptop away after nine o'clock and come to bed with me for some good old fashioned 'connection' with your husband.
SARAH I think I could be persuaded *(she kisses him again)* I've not seen your 'hard drive' for a while, or pressed your buttons come to that. And I've got some good news too.
KEVIN Oh? And what would that be?
SARAH Well, we're going to be hearing the patter of tiny feet.
KEVIN *(Confused)* What? Are we getting another dog?
SARAH *(Smiling)* No, I think we have our hands full with the mutt we've got.
KEVIN *(Horrified)* Oh no! You're getting Gerbils!!
SARAH *(Playfully punches his arm)* No, guess again.
KEVIN Er, a horse?
SARAH No silly, god you can be silly at times. *(indicates her tummy)* I'm pregnant!
KEVIN *(shocked)* Pregnant? Wow!! *(he breaks away)* Hang on, for how long?
SARAH Three months now. I've been for my scan today and everything's okay.
KEVIN Why didn't you tell me sooner?
SARAH I was afraid to. I didn't know how you would react. I mean, we haven't exactly been getting on lately have we?
KEVIN Wow! That's bloody great news! After all the 'trying' we've been doing as well. Hang on.
SARAH What?
KEVIN Well, we've hardly had sex the last few months what with me sleeping in the back room.
SARAH Oh it's yours alright. Remember the night you came back from the gym and boasted that you were shagging Leanne?
KEVIN Er, not really.

SARAH You was pissed. Anyway, that night we, you know and er, here I am, finally pregnant after all the 'trying' that we've had. Maybe you should come home paralytic more often.

She hugs him, taking him by surprise.

KEVIN I vaguely remember that night. I thought I was dreaming it.
SARAH *(Cheerfully)* Believe me, you weren't dreaming!
KEVIN But you weren't with me when I woke up.
SARAH I sneaked back to my bed just as you were stirring. I heard you coming upstairs whingeing to yourself as you usually do and I waited until I knew you would be nearly asleep and then I sneaked into your bed. Anyway, you were well horny that night and so was I, and you know what?
KEVIN I don't know? What?
SARAH It was amazing! I like it when you're half in dream land and half pissed, you relax more. And you know something else?
KEVIN I dunno, what?
SARAH I enjoyed it. Even though I knew you hated me, but it was great! Just like the old days. I felt like I was being sneaky but I was well horny that night I must admit and you didn't let me down at all. And you know something else?
KEVIN *(rolling his eyes in mock annoyance)* No, I don't. Pray tell.
SARAH Well, I can't believe I wasted so much of my time on a computer playing games for the last five months when I could have been having so much fun playing with you and your joystick

Kevin happily hugs her and they happily kiss.

KEVIN If you put it like that I don't mind you playing with it either! Welcome back
SARAH Oh, do me a favour tomorrow will you?
KEVIN What's that?
SARAH Hide that damn laptop somewhere in the house where I won't find it.
KEVIN I've got a better idea.
SARAH What?
KEVIN Let's just put it in the bin eh?
SARAH Nooo, don't be silly, I know you've been dying to check out all those porn sites for ages, what are they? Red Tube, Brazzers, Pink Elephant

and Devil Tube? Why should I deprive you of your fun? But you won't need them now will you?

KEVIN *(Embarrassed)* Yeah, but they're porn sites. I can't go on them, it's not right.

SARAH Who am I to say what's wrong or right? I quite like the thought of you watching porn and then getting horny so you can show me some new tricks you've learned.

KEVIN Are you having me on? You want me to watch porn and you're not bothered?

SARAH I'm *your wife* Kevin, you have no secrets from me. We have no secrets have we?

KEVIN *(unsure)* Okay, I'm banged to rights. Yes I have wanted to watch porn, I can't deny it.

SARAH I know, I've seen you mag stash.

KEVIN *(embarrassed)* Ahh, er, sorry.

SARAH I don't mind, honestly *(she kisses him)* Promise me one thing though.

KEVIN What? Anything for you my mummy to be.

SARAH You will only go on porn sites? You won't go on Facebook?

KEVIN You're sure you don't mind me going onto porn sites? Wow, I wish every wife was like you. *(he looks her in the eye and becomes serious)* I cannot promise you anything like that whatsoever. I mean, Facebook has had you in its mighty grip for so long I think I might sign up and become your friend and we can have 'online' chats while I'm upstairs in the bedroom and you are down here eating yourself to death. What do you think?

She looks at him as if she will hit him as his face is non-committal. Then she realises he is joking as he can't keep a straight face and laughs. She playfully hits him as he heartily laughs.

KEVIN Ha ha! Gotcha!!

THE END

About the Author

Robert Goodier was born, grew up, lives and still hangs around Bolton. His hobbies/interests/lifetime vocations, should he win the National Lottery, are playing guitar, writing songs, singing songs, recording songs, writing poetry, acting in plays and writing plays, alongside boring stuff like reading and going to the cinema a lot (plus watching films while lounging around in bed munching chocolates and quaffing red wine) Also, he has four very excellent poetry books published alongside a selection of his best stage plays (a selection of published titles is listed overleaf). Many many years ago he was a presenter for Radio Bolton in 1995 and a Saturday DJ for Bolton Market Radio from October 1999 to May 2001 (in which he played Slade's "Merry Xmas Everybody" six times in one show and nobody noticed). In recent years he has merrily been inflicting his singing voice and guitar playing on unsuspecting audiences at various Open Mic Nights in venues that will let him in. He rents a house, doesn't have a car and has never considered wearing a wig.

Other plays by the author

Ghost Of Thornley Hall in Cumbria

Retired Detective Inspector Mr. Armani and his wife are invited by a long forgotten relative to stay the weekend at his Cumbrian mansion for the reading of a will, he is not expecting the 'eccentricities' of the relatives and other guests. Nor is he expecting the tale of a ghost of the first Earl of Thornley to be so prominent. But it is the three hundredth anniversary of his death and his ghost still haunts the house! Mr. Armani is in no mood for the hidden treasure or the attempts to find it. Neither is he in the mood for Timpkins the frustrated and annoying butler, Edna the maid who will 'dress up' for the Earl, Mabel the sex mad niece, Kipling the dodgy tenant or the newly wed Mr and Mrs Winsome. In fact he wants to relax, but everybody - and his wife - have different ideas!

To Be Announced

Do you ever wonder how a successful amateur dramatics society is run? Who casts the parts and chooses the seasons plays? Well this hilarious play takes you behinds the scenes of a squabbling society with two of the main protagonists fighting it out to be the head honcho.

Alice is opposed to Maggie, who for years has been trying to persuade her society to stage one of the many plays that she's written, but Alice is Chairwoman and has the final say; which is always 'No' Matters come to a head after a heated argument when Maggie is booted out from the society and out of spite they both stage a play at the same time in a battle of supremacy. Who wins? The audience does! So come along, buy a front row seat and take a peek inside as the battle rages...

Family Revelations

Maureen Jackman is a tyrant, she rules over her ex-husband Colin with a hard fist and takes no nonsense from her son Leonard who she thinks is going to get engaged to the daughter of the richest family In town. But at a party that she insists on having, she meets Leonard's bride to be and her family's eccentric lifestyle that opens her eyes, making her realise that being an old 'fuddy duddy' is out of sorts with the world as she realises her son isn't the man she thought she was.

Murderous Intentions

Alistair and Martine Richmond live in their sprawling country mansion near Chorley Lancashire and have buried their daughter who had drowned two weeks before. On the evening of the funeral strange things happen to the housekeeper in the kitchen and who is the mysterious figure in the grounds looking at the house? And why has Charles Richmond been locked in his suddenly freezing Arctic bedroom for the night? The next day all is revealed by an unexpected visitor. . . . who reveals secrets the Richmond family desperately tried to hide from each other and changes their lives. Forever.

Perfect Suspect

Marcus Winstanley inherits a vast fortune from an extremely rich uncle and while going through his uncles possessions he finds a cassette tape in a locked case with his name on it, dated 25 years previous. Curious, he listens to the tape to discover that his uncle was discussing to another man about having him killed should he not get married or if he did his wife did not bear him a son. This completely stuns him, as the tape also states the name of his wife *and* the name of his daughter and also a *date* on which he would be murdered by the mystery man on the tape. The news upsets him and Police Inspectors Turner and Glover do not reassure him with their confidence either! Not only that, but the news of the Will also upsets his brother, who tended to his uncle in his last years and he is annoyed that he doesn't get a penny *and* add to the fact that the recording of his dead uncle's Will states that Marcus has two weeks left to live; the race is on to halt his ultimate demise!

www.ingramcontent.com/pod-product-compliance
Ingram Content Group UK Ltd.
Pitfield, Milton Keynes, MK11 3LW, UK
UKHW020234250726
13967UKWH00001B/356